DAILY JOURNAL

This Book Belongs To

....

There's nothing quite like opening a new journal and sitting down in your special place to write.

Research shows that journaling can help you achieve your goals, increase your emotional intelligence, boost your confidence, heal & grow and even form the base to write your own book.

But what do I write about?

When you're feeling overwhelmed or not sure what direction to take, pausing for a moment to reflect can be a very powerful exercise. By asking yourself questions and writing the answers, will help you move forward. Even when the answer is unclear, writing or drawing something can often release anxiety and put things into perspective.

This journal will help you through a variety of daily exercises. Choose which are relevant to you, or skip them entirely if you feel compelled to explore your own ideas.

Whatever you choose, you have already started upon your journey, congratulations

In this moment, what are four things I am grateful for?

1)

2)

3)

4)

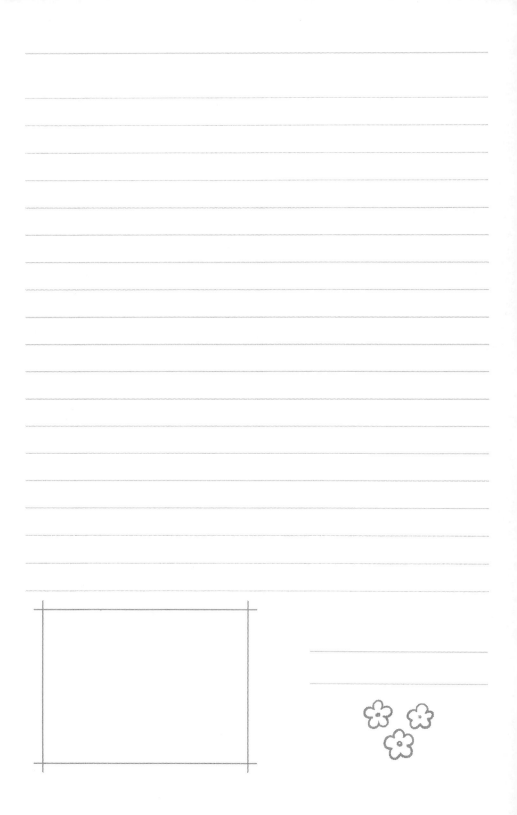

What four things do I like about myself?

1)

2)

3)

4)

What four things do I not like about myself?

1)

2)

3)

4)

What makes me happy?

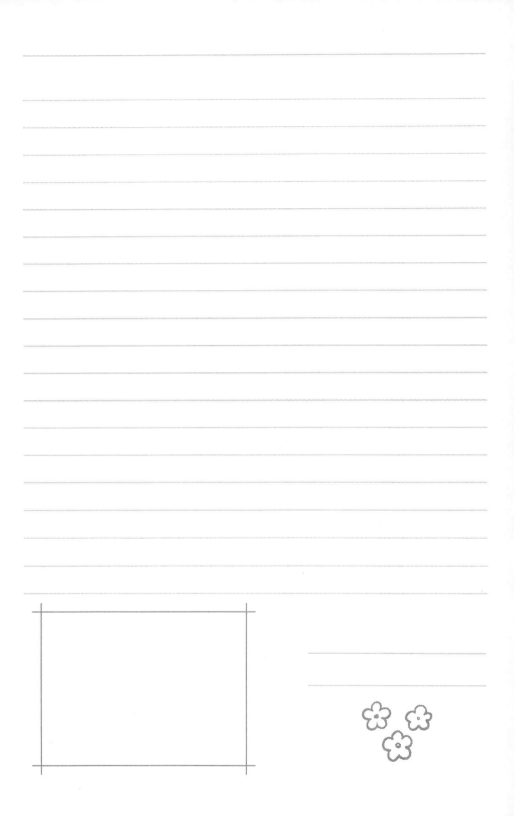

What beliefs do I have which prevent me reaching my goals?

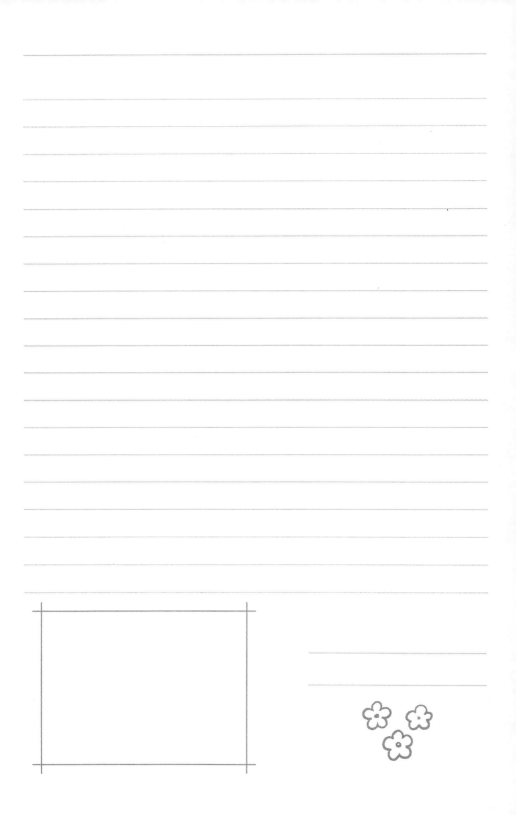

When do I feel most in tune with myself?

What are 10 goals I want to reach this year?

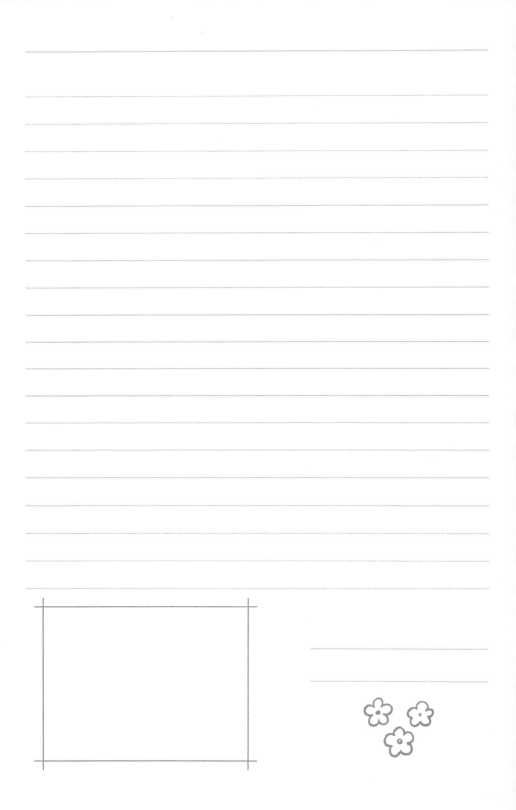

If I could take advice from my younger self. What would it be?

_____

_____

_____

_____

_____

_____

_____

_____

_____

_____

_____

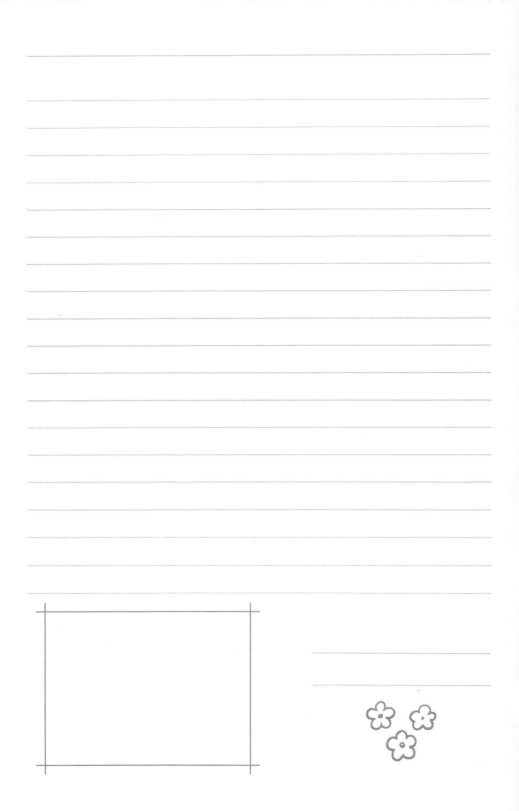

Where do I see myself in 5 years time?

Where do I see myself in 10 years time?

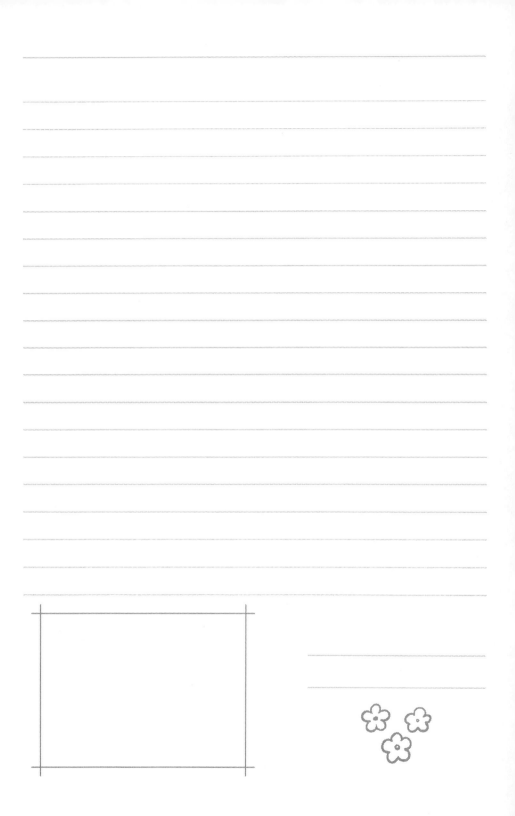

What will I do in the next year to achieve my goals?

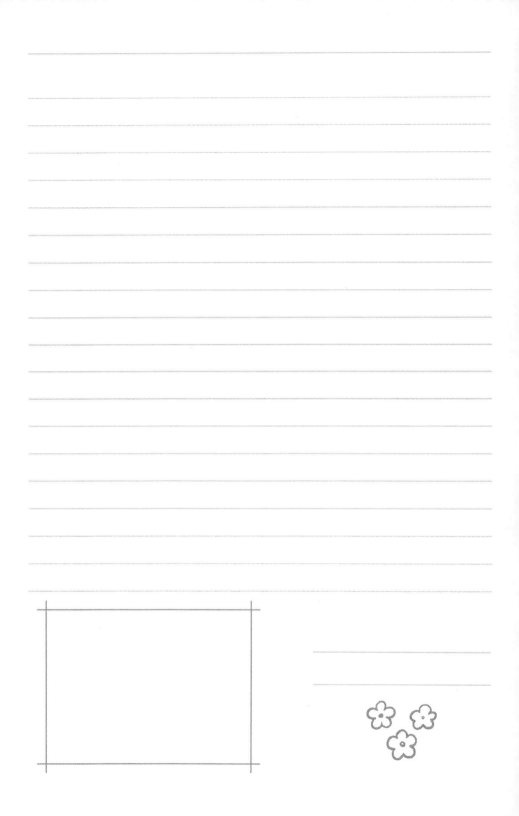

Use the following pages to note your daily thoughts and feelings. Feel free to write, draw or stick items of importance

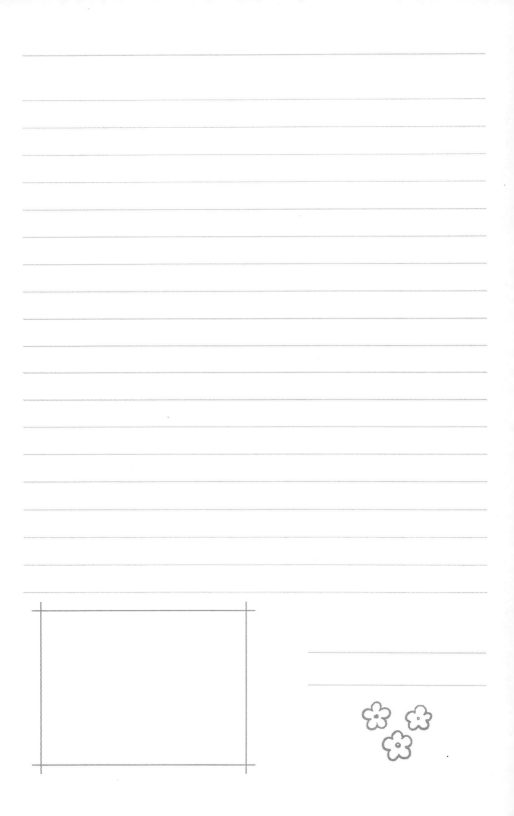

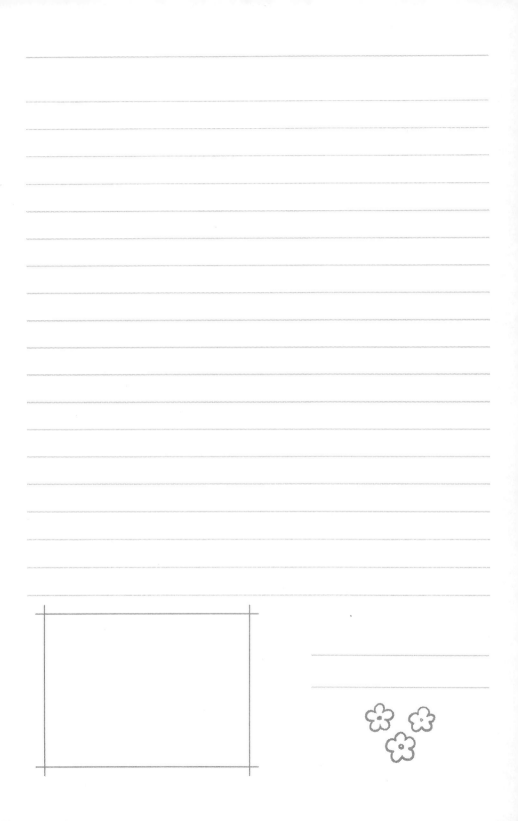

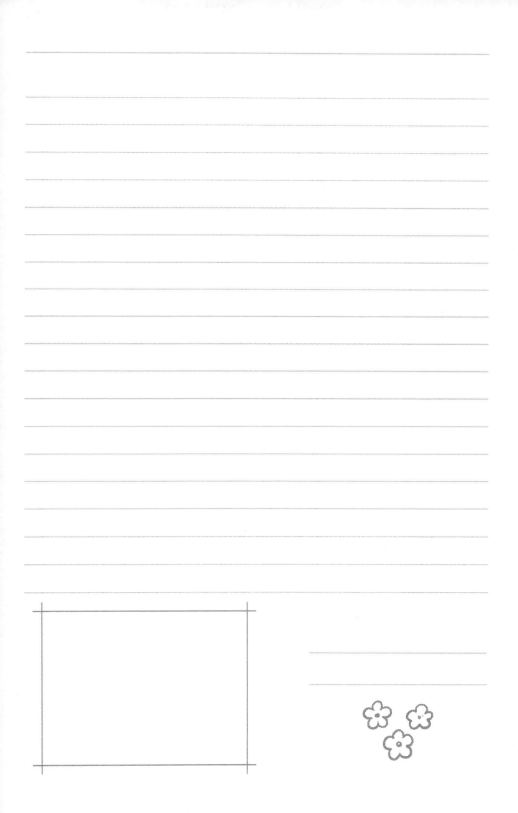

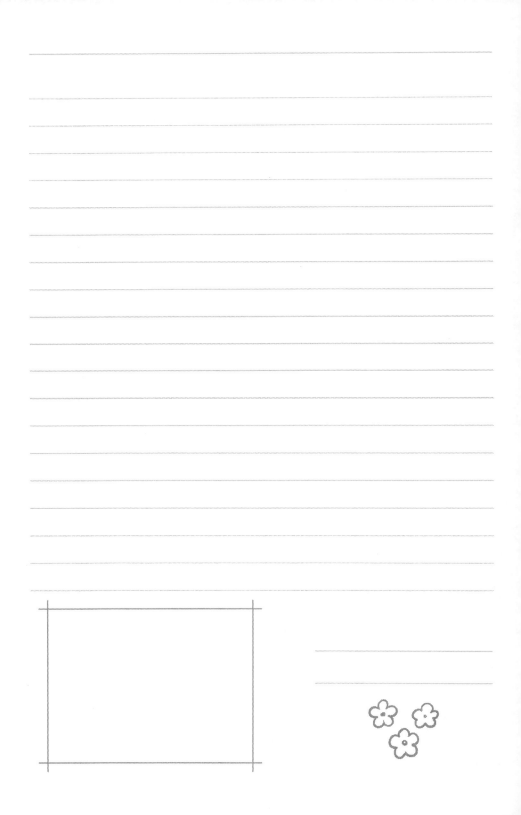

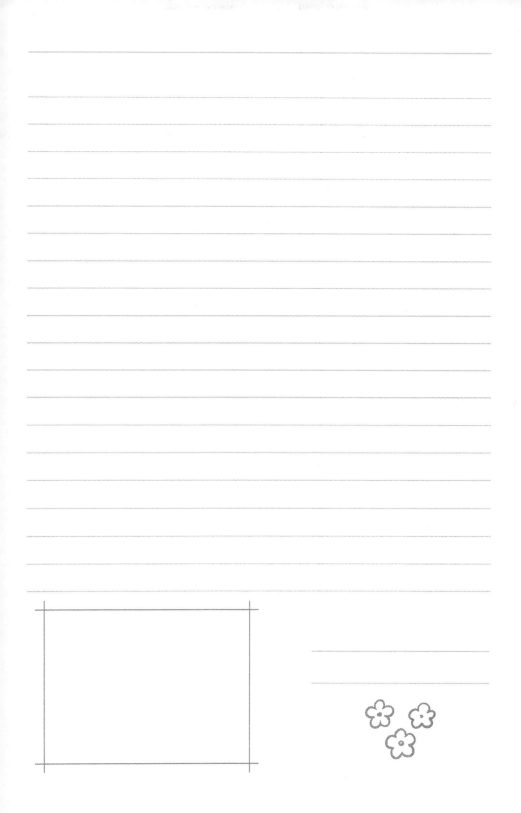

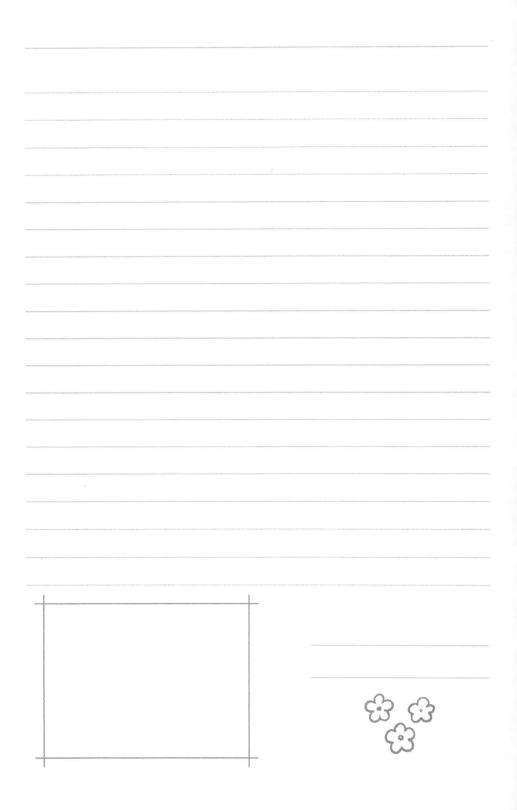

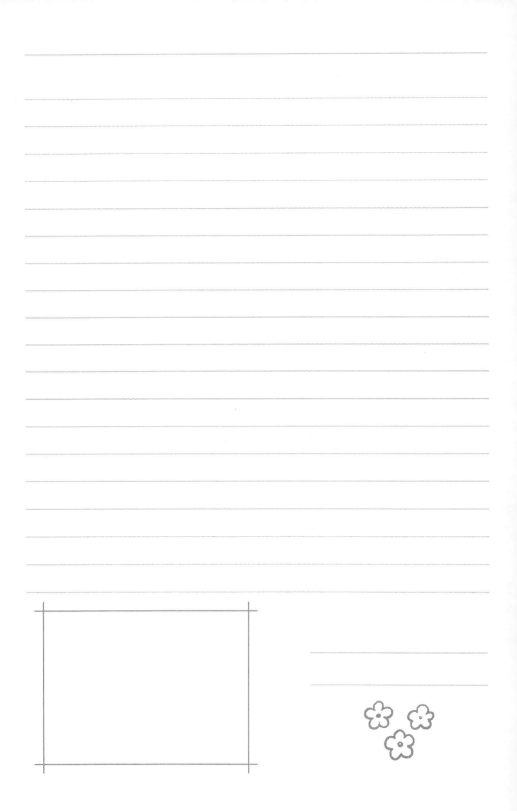

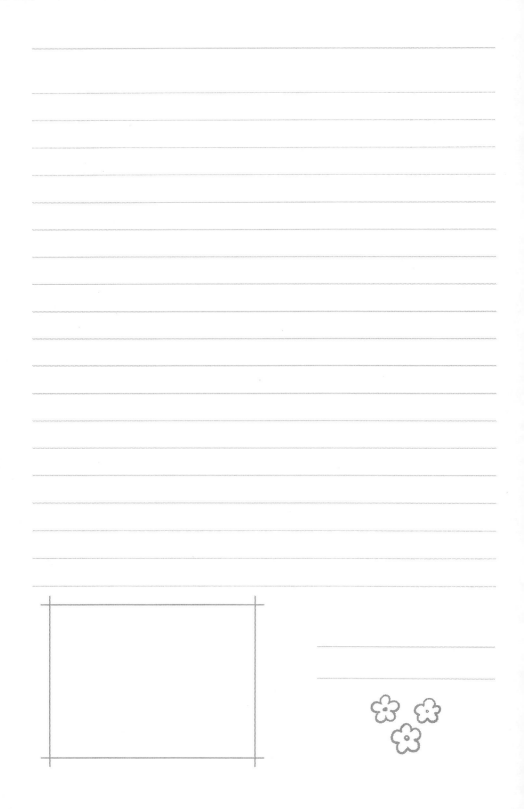

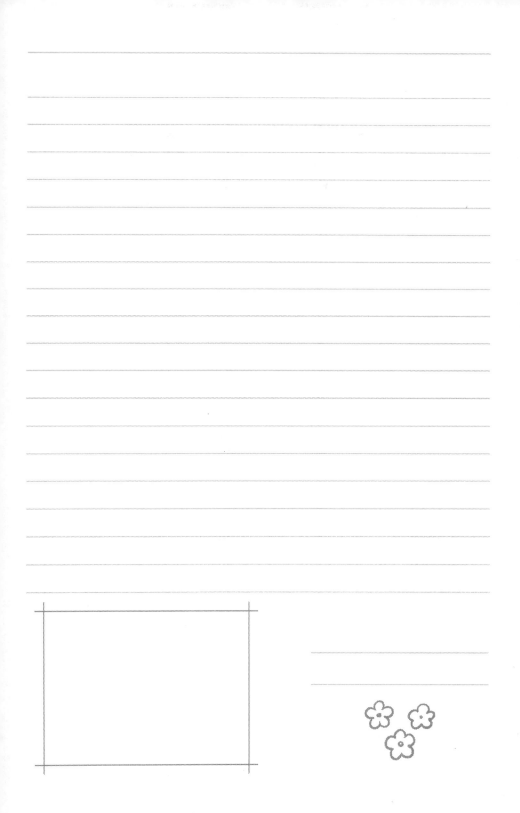

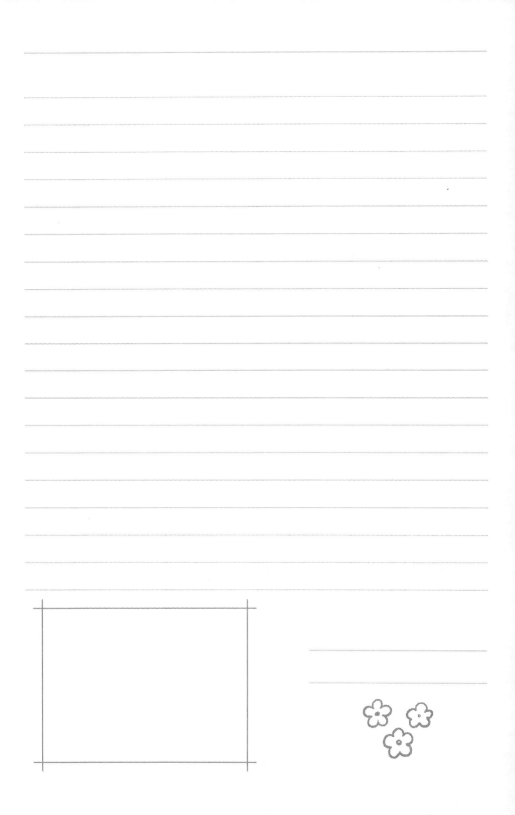

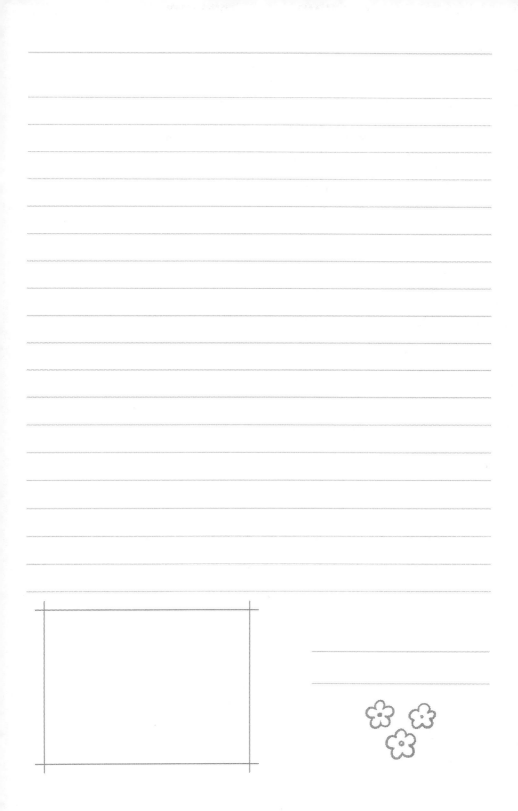

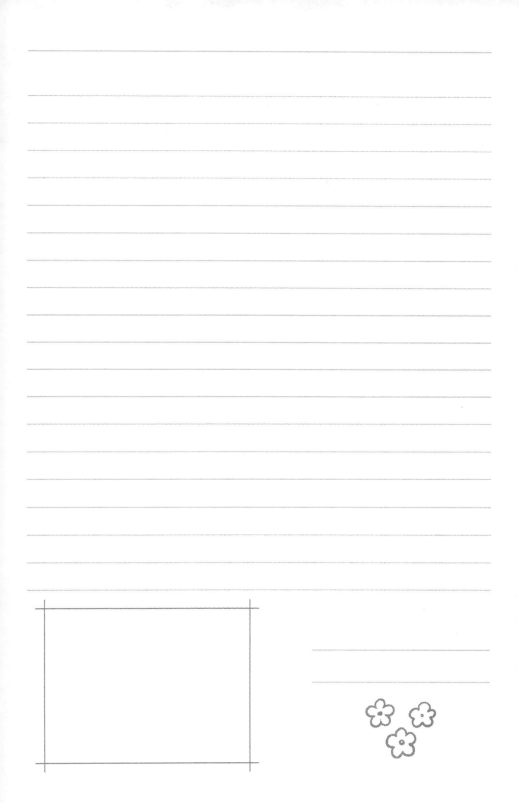

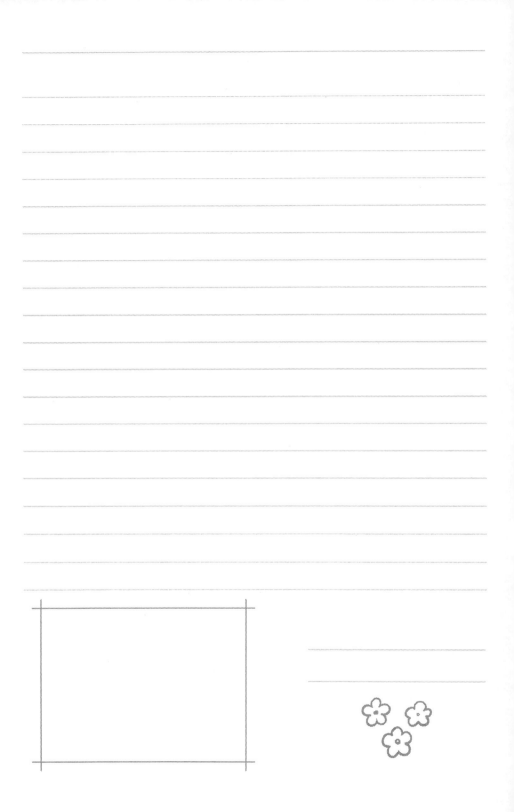

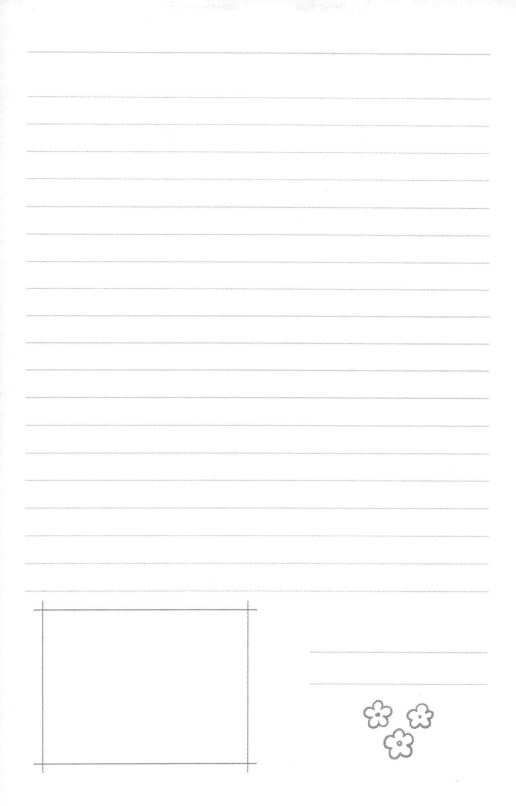

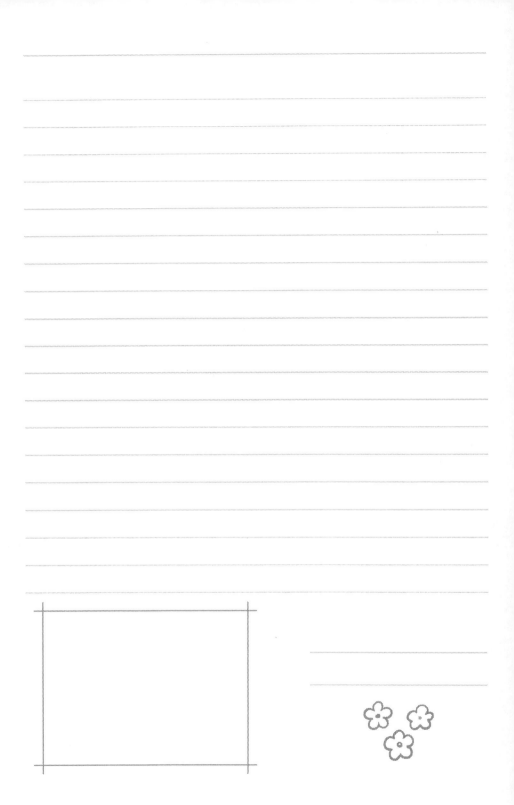

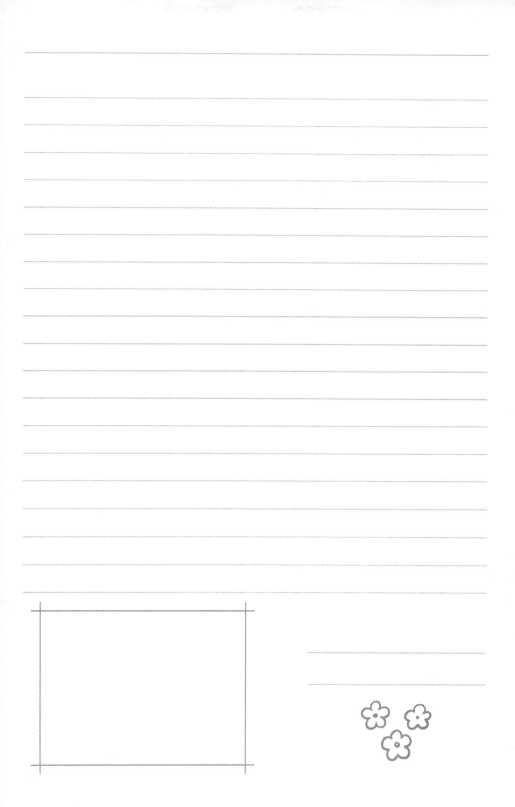

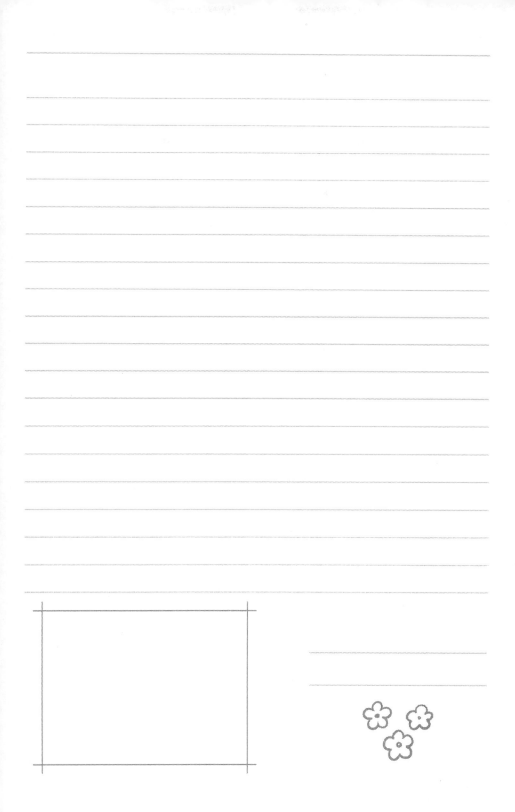

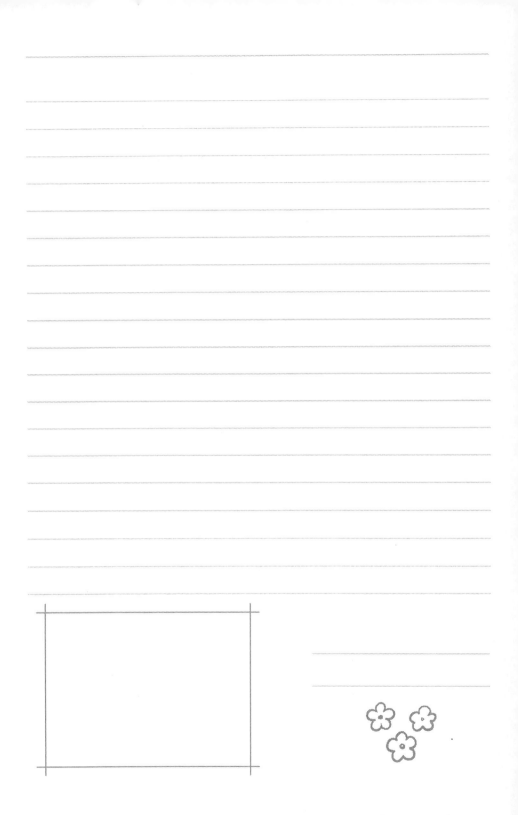

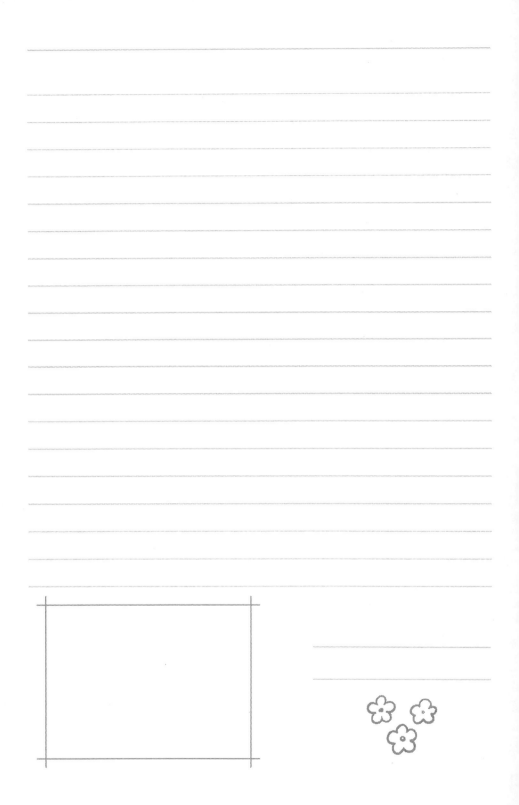

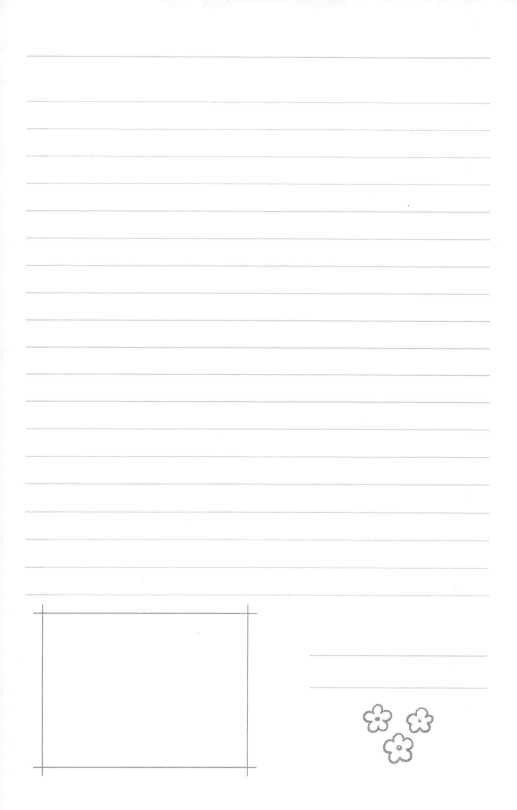

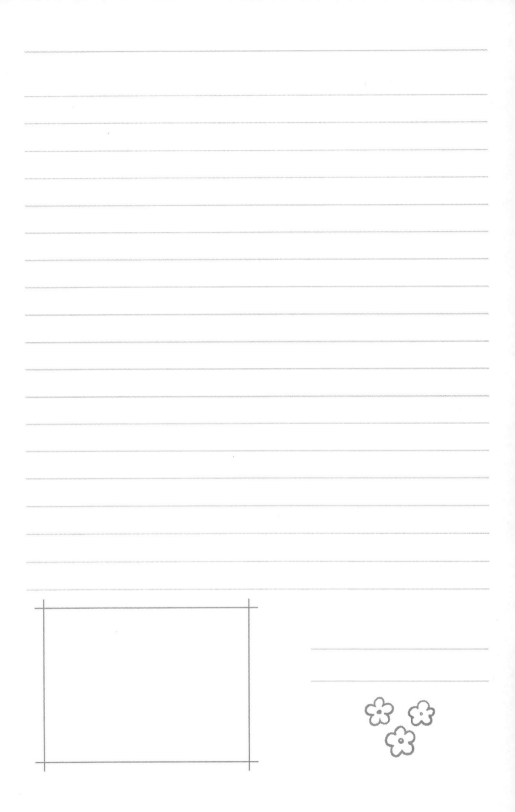

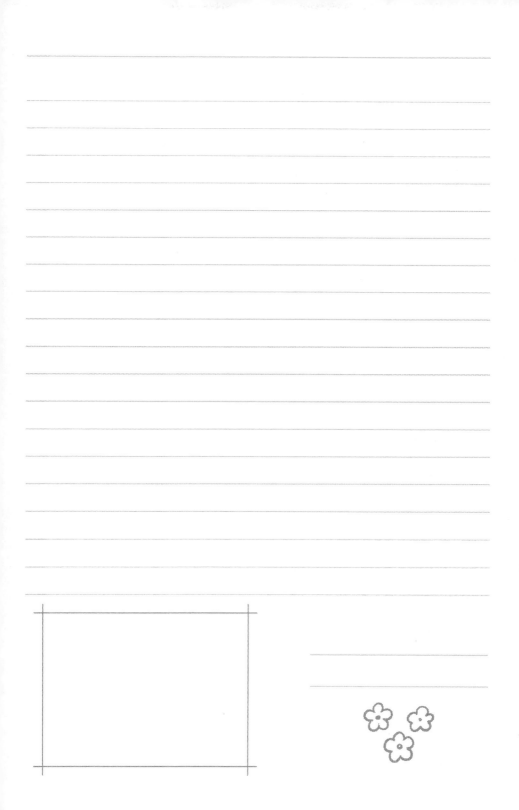

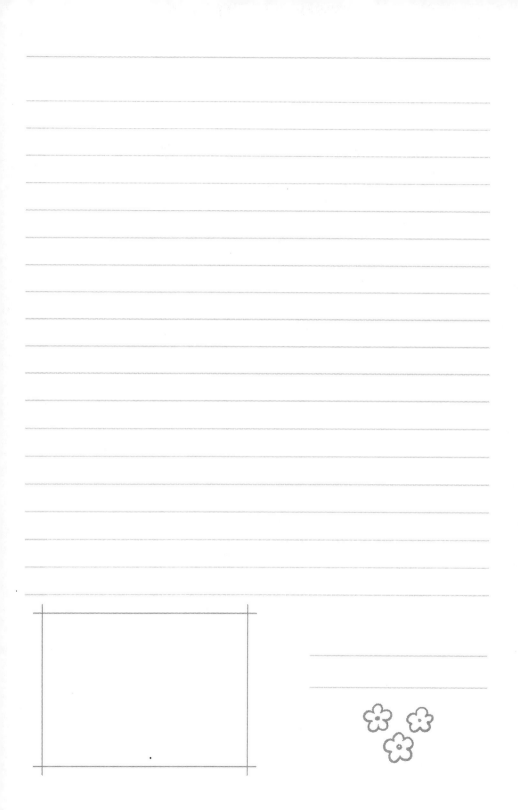

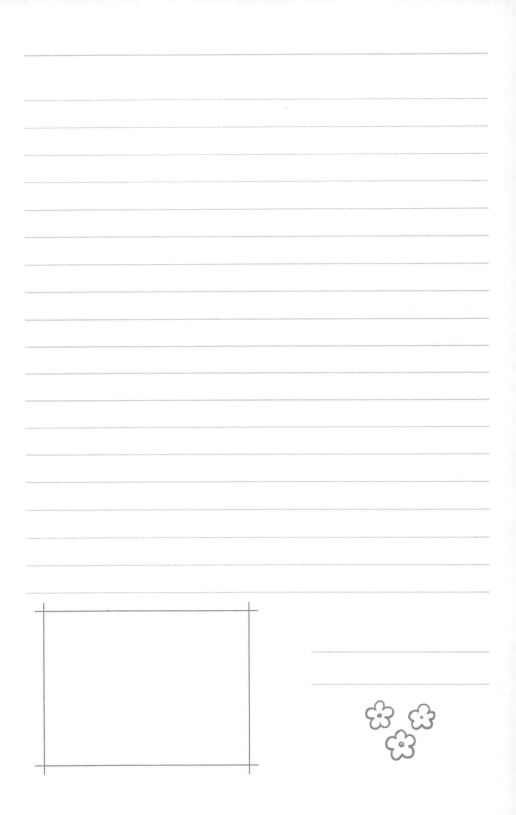

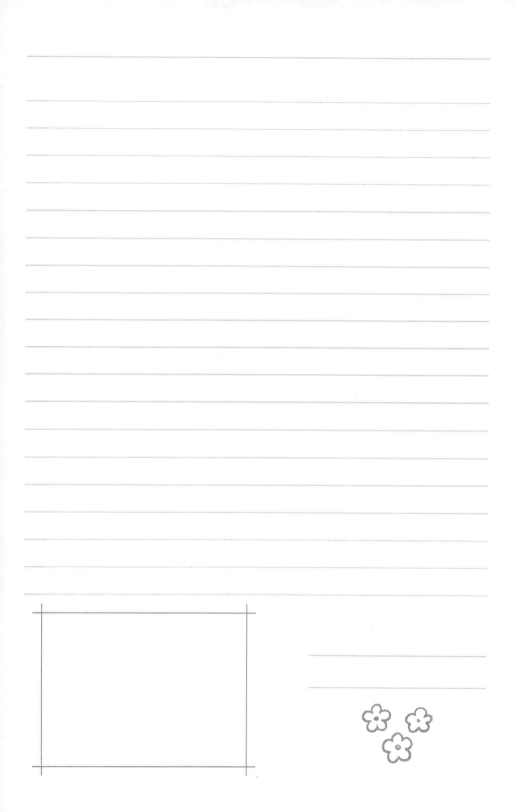

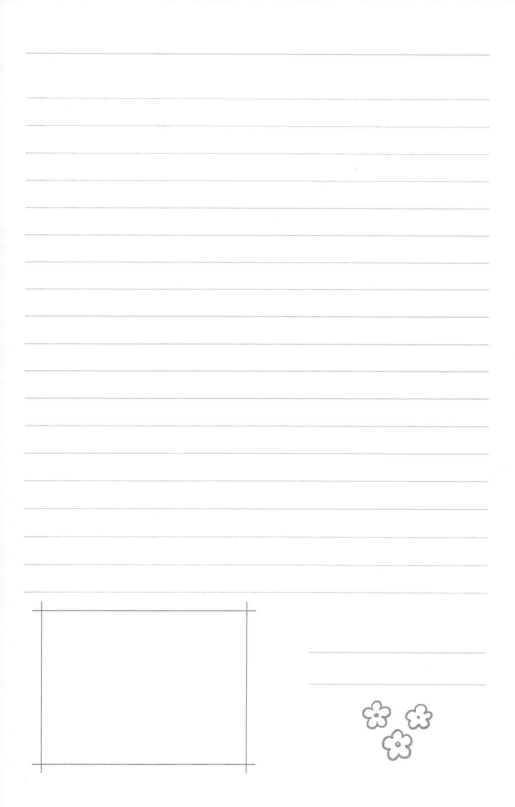

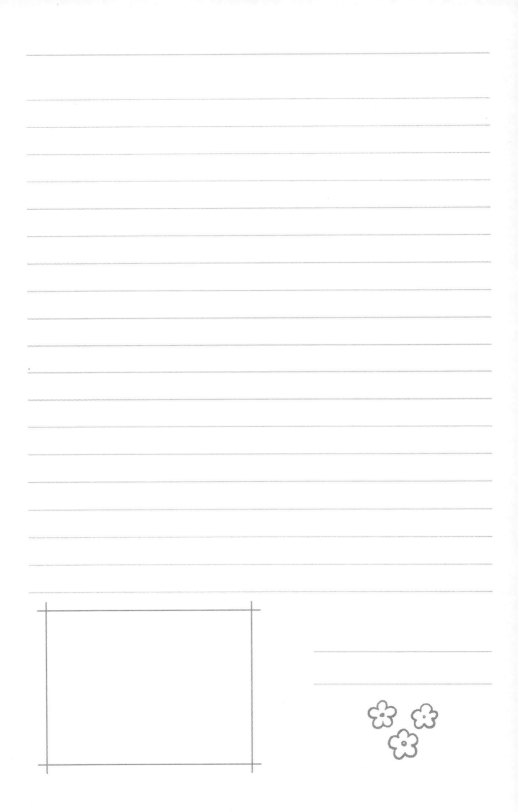

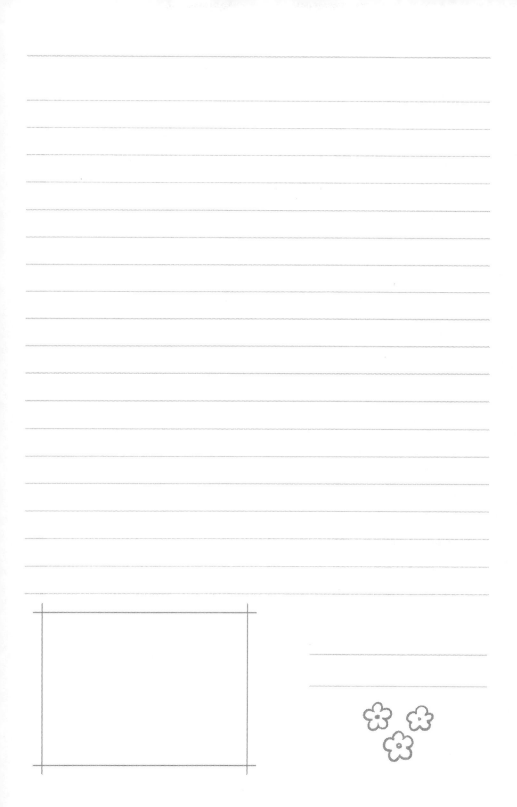

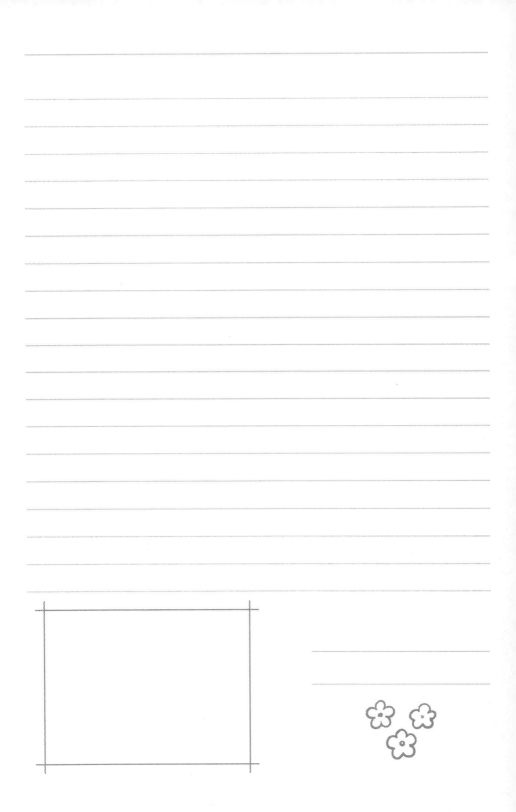

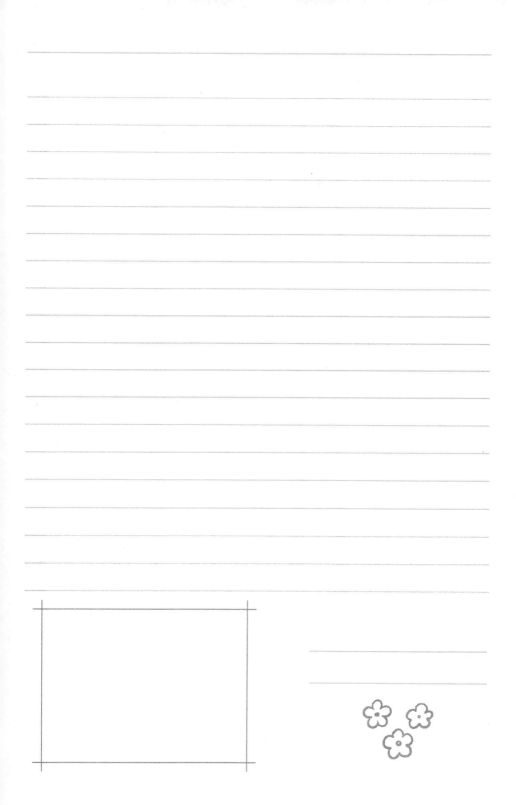

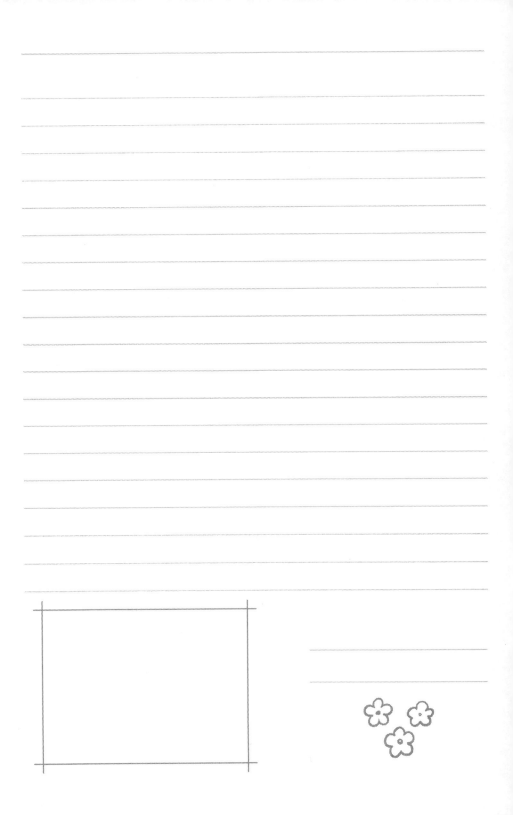

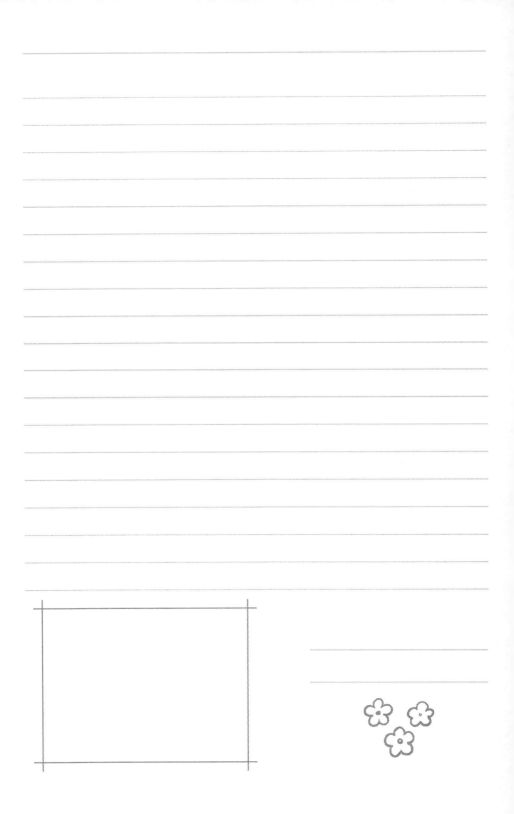

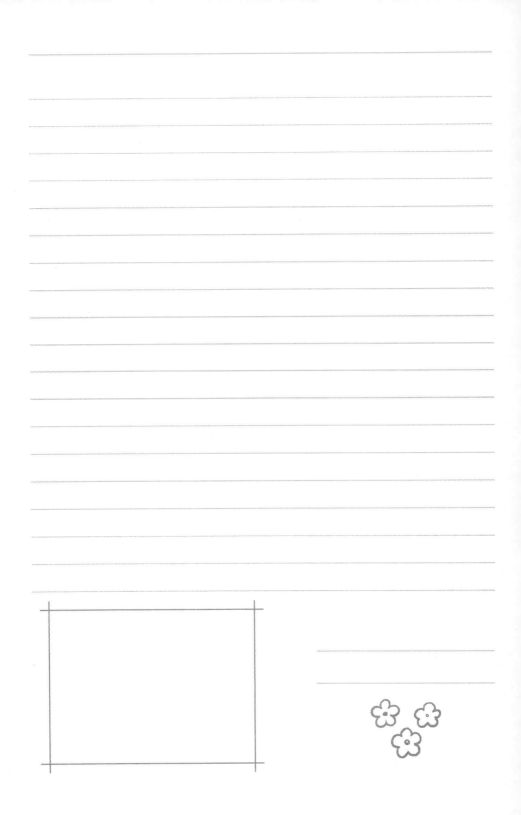

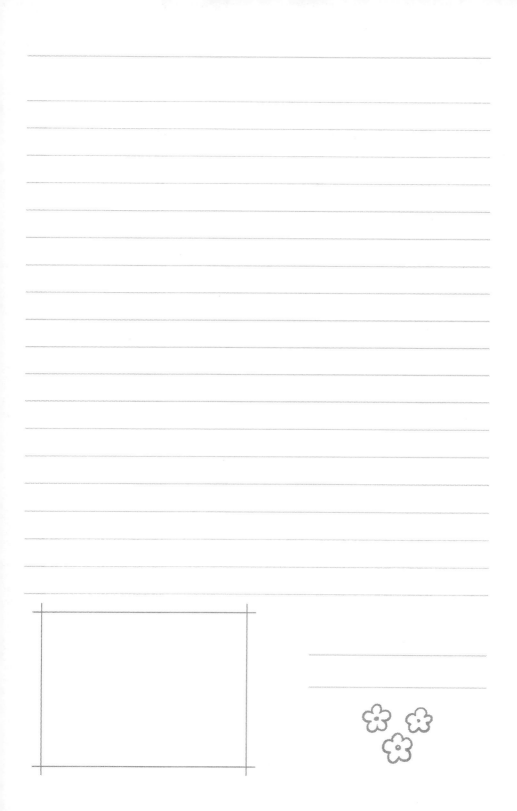

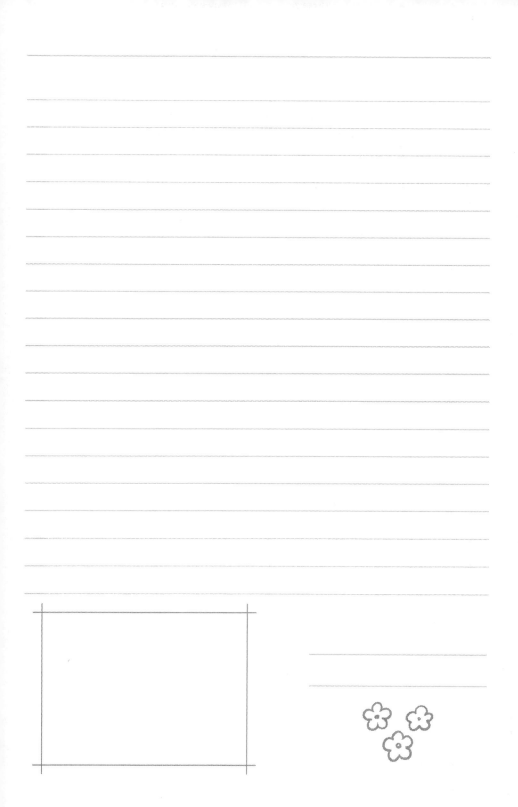

Take a look back at your answers to the questions at the begining of this book. Are your answers different to what you think now?

Printed in Great Britain
by Amazon